A Caterpillar Singing Loudly

A Yoga Book

inspired by The Twelve Days of Christmas that can be used all year round.

Written by *Joanna Bertzeletos*

Photographer *Sarah Ingolfsdottir*
Illustrations and costume design *Ruthie Ford*
Face Painting *Liz Searle*
Graphic Design *Jason Major*

Published by Yoga Nature Sheffield
First Edition, November 2011.

Printed in United Kingdom

A CIP record for this book is available from the
British Library.

Printed by Northend Creative Print Solutions
www.northend.co.uk

ISBN 978-0-9570810-0-0

Contents

Starring...

Here are the children who will guide you through the sequence. They will show you how to do each of the postures in the sequence and later they will show you some others you may wish to explore.

Caitlin as the Caterpillar.

Lily as the Cobra.

Sophia as the Dormouse.

Francesca as the Happy Cat.

Elise as the Downward Dog.

Morgan as the Crazy Lizard.

Hayden as the Swan.

Cenya as the Camel.

Sahara as the Cheetah.

Resian as the Tree.

Jonny as the Surfer.

Alexandra as the Dancer.

About This Book

Respecting your body

Before going on your yogic adventure it is important that you respect your body and honour its needs. If you have any health conditions or are uncertain as to whether or not you can do the postures or the sequence in this book please make sure you speak to someone in the medical profession and/or an appropriately trained yoga instructor.

Who is this book for?

This book can be used by anyone from as young as 3 years of age to grown-up age. I have had the great honour of sharing "A Caterpillar Singing Loudly" with a great variety of groups. I have taught it in Montissori, Primary and Secondary Schools, with both children and adults with Special Needs and with my various adult groups. The main criteria is to have fun with it and not to worry too much about alignment as the more you practice it the more your body will click into place.

How to use this book?

Even though this book is based on "The Twelve Days of Christmas" it can actually be used at any time of the year. I have written the book in a way to enable this to happen. However, when it is close to the Festive season around November time you simply change "on the first day I met him" to "on the first day of Christmas" and then you can do the sequence over the festive period.

Word box

Sequence - A sequence is when you put things in order. You can have number sequences, shape sequences, dance sequences or yoga sequences.

Transition - A transition is how you get from one stage to the next or from one step to the next. In this case it is how you change from one posture into the next.

Alignment - Alignment simply means making sure that you or things are not crooked.

The book has been laid out into the following eight sections:

- *Shake and Wake Up* – here you will find three simple moves to prepare your body for the sequence.

- *Becoming a Grand Master Yogini or Yogi* – in this section you will focus on mastering each of the 12 postures in the sequence. To help you they have been colour coded.

- *How do I Get From One Pose to the Next* – in this section you will find guidance on the transition stages, that is, how to get from one pose to the next.

- *A Caterpillar Singing Loudly The full Sequence* – here you have an overview of the sequence where you can put all you have learnt together.

- *Some other Asanas you may wish to try* – once you have mastered the postures in the sequence you may wish to try some other yoga poses.

- *Yogic Nap Time (Yoga Nidra)* – in this section you will find guidance on how to go into a deep relaxation.

- *Facts about A Caterpillar Singing Loudly* – here you will find interesting facts about how many postures you end up doing when you do the sequence once.

- *Goodbye* – here you will say farewell to the Caterpillar Singing Loudly gang and you will find out how old they are and why they like yoga.

Throughout the book you will find projects to do, interesting vocabulary, ways to empower yourself and how to get your body into a variety of yoga shapes. For some of the activities described in this book you may need someone to help you and besides it is always nice to share your yoga practice with someone.

What is yoga?

Yoga is a very old form of exercise that comes from India. People called archaeologists believe it may go back as far as 6000 years. The word yoga means "yoke", to stick together two halves, to make you feel whole. What am I talking about? When you are sat in a classroom and a teacher is going blah, blah, blah, blah, your body is there in the classroom but your mind is elsewhere as you think about rainbows, fairies, goblins and dragons and on top of that you may be feeling a little bit sad. At that moment your body, mind and emotions are not stuck together, they are all doing different things. By doing yoga you will yoke yourself together and be able to concentrate more and be more happy.

Why is yoga good?

Yoga is not like regular exercise. You get to turn your body into funny shapes, called "Asanas". Asana is Sanskrit for posture. Most of the Asanas are based on animals (cheetah, swan, cobra etc), geometry (pose of eight points or caterpillar), warriors (surfer dude or dudess), plants (trees) and heroes (dancer). It is fun, easy to do and will help you to relax. It will also help you to get in touch with your feelings, teach you how to interact with other people, you will learn strange names for different parts of your body, and it will help you with balance, concentration, flexibility and strength.

What is Sanskrit?

The word yoga actually comes from a language that is as old as the exercise itself called Sanskrit. We have already used two Sanskrit words. Can you guess which ones they were? Yes, that's right yoga and asana. Through this book I will also give you the Sanskrit name for the Asanas. So you will be yoking yourself together and learning a very old and mystical language. You are bound to develop some sort of super power, I am sure of it!

Important Tip! Back and forward bends always go together!

After a strong back bend like cobra or camel it is important to do some forward bends, like…

Dormouse
Child Pose, Balasana
(Bala = Child and Asana = Pose)

→

Sad Cat,
Cat Pose, Marjaryasana
(Marjari = Cat and Asana = Pose)

Tips for a fun and safe yogic adventure!

- Make sure you have a safe and quiet space to practice your yoga in;

- Wear comfortable clothes and take your socks off;

- Try not to eat too much before your practice;

- Yoga is meant to be fun so don't take it too seriously;

- If you fall out of a pose make sure you have a hearty laugh;

- The more you practice the easier it becomes;

- Remember to breathe deeply and fully through the nose (not the mouth unless you are told to do this or you have a blocked nose);

- After your practice drink some water and have a healthy snack.

Word box

Here are some words that might help you with your project. If you think of other words make sure you write them down!

Tired, stressed, strong, relaxed, flexible, taller, happy, sad, angry, lost, confused, racing, negative, bad, positive, good, peaceful, content, low, dull, blue.

Project:

Equipment - Get some paper, scissors, glue, felt tips, post-it notes and some old nature magazines.

Create – a poster of all the postures you are going to work with over the weeks. On your poster mark which postures you are going to work with today.

Post-it – on your post-it notes write the answers to the following questions…

Answer these questions before you do the yoga –

1. How does my body feel now?

2. Do I feel happy, sad, angry, cross, confused or anything else you may be feeling?

3. What are my thoughts doing? Are they racing? Are they positive thoughts?

4. What is my energy like?

Answer these questions after you do the yoga –

1. Does my body feel different compared to before I had done this posture?

2. Have my feelings changed?

3. How does my brain feel?

4. What is my energy like?

Wake And Shake Up

Before we go on our yogic adventure it is important to get our bodies prepared by doing a "wake and shake up". Here you will find three simple movements to help you get your body ready. Put on your favourite funky tune and move to its groove with the following moves… be creative, mix and match and don't forget to make up your own!

The Jelly-Monster Shake

You are made of jelly and you begin to shake your hands, then your arms, then one leg and the next until you are shaking like a Jelly-Monster. Shake to the sky, shake to the earth, lye on your back and shake faster than the speed of light!

I am the wind

Imagine that your arms are like that of a scarecrow and the wind begins to blow through them. First they fly around your hips uncontrollably, then up to your shoulders and then right over your head. You have turned into a tornado. Keep swinging your arms up around you like a tornado. How long can you do it for?

Criss-Cross Double Time

A really good one to get your brain hooked up. Start off really S L O W by taking your right hand to your left knee and then your left hand to your right knee. Have I confused you already? Make sure you are creating a diagonal with your hand and knee. You start off slow, you speed up until you are doing Criss-Cross Double Time. Now for a bit of fun see if you can do the same but elbow to knee. Too easy for you? Then what about a diagonal high kick?

Why is it good?

- Muscles get warmed before doing the Asanas;
- The brain gets ready to do more complicated things;
- It helps to get rid of any bad parts of your day.

A Caterpillar Singing Loudly Overview

Here is an overview of the sequence you are going to learn in this book. Please do cut out this poster and put it on your wall so that you can practice the sequence with ease. Before moving on to doing the postures on the other side of this poster it is recommended that you practice this side first as explained in the instructions of this book.

On the first day I met him
my yogi sent to me
a caterpillar singing loudly.

On the second day I met him
my yogi sent to me
two hissing cobras.

On the third day I met him
my yogi sent to me
three stretched out dormice.

On the fourth day I met him
my yogi sent to me
four happy cats.

On the fifth day I met him
my yogi sent to me
five downward dogs.

On the sixth day I met him
my yogi sent to me
six crazy lizards.

On the seventh day I met him
my yogi sent to me
seven swans-a-swimming.

On the eighth day I met him
my yogi sent to me
eight festive camels.

On the ninth day I met him
my yogi sent to me
nine cheetahs running.

On the tenth day I met him
my yogi sent to me
ten trees-a-swaying.

On the eleventh day I met him
my yogi sent to me
eleven surfers surfing.

On the twelfth day I met him
my yogi sent to me
twelve dancers dancing.

…a caterpillar singing loudly

…two hissing cobras

…three stretched-out dormice

…four happy cats

…five downward-dogs

…six crazy lizards

…seven swans-a-swimming

…eight festive camels

…nine cheetahs running

…ten trees-a-swaying

… eleven surfers surfing

… twelve dancers dancing

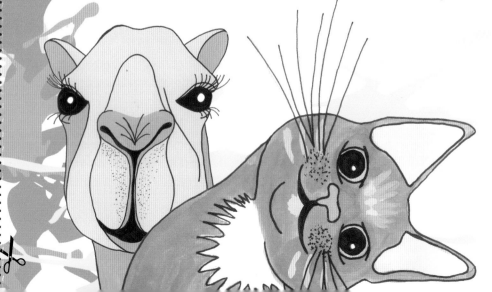

1

…a caterpillar singing loudly

2

…two hissing cobras

3

…three stretched-out dormouse

4

… four happy cats

5

…five downward-dogs

6

… six crazy lizards

7

… seven swans-a-swimming

8

… eight festive camels

9

…nine cheetahs running

10

… ten trees-a-swaying

11

…eleven surfers surfing

12

…twelve dancers dancing

Becoming A Grand Master Yogini Or Yogi

Now it is time to start our yogic adventure. The following section has been divided into two pages. On the left hand page is the photo of the child or children in makeup with the "starring" child of that posture wearing a costume. On the right hand page is the "starring" child of that posture showing you how to go into the pose in stages. Master these ones before you try the varieties that the other children are demonstrating on the left hand page. Take your time and master them well as this will help you to flow when you are ready to do the full sequence – A Caterpillar Singing Loudly. You will then be a true Grand Master Yogini or Yogi!

In this section the focus is very much on learning each of the postures so it is a nice idea to hold the posture for a while, focus on your breath and see how it makes you feel.

Project 1

Write down your dreams, your goals. At the start of either the school year or new year. Don't make the list too big. What would you like to achieve?

- *Pass an exam?*
- *Go to a different school?*
- *Help someone?*
- *Global Peace?*
- *Get a special gift for either yourself or someone else?*

Write them down or if you are feeling really creative you may want to make a collage that you can put on your wall so every morning you can be reminded. If you are making a collage you may also want to include pictures of how you might achieve that dream. What steps can you make to get a little bit closer to it? Most of the time you will achieve what you have written down or on your collage but sometimes your dream may take longer than a year to achieve so just carry it over into the next year.

Project 2

Setting an Intention

A really nice thing to do before you start practicing your yoga postures is that you set an intention. Think of only one thing that you would like to achieve or change

for example –

- *Are your thoughts sometimes bad and would you like to change them to good thoughts?*
- *Is there something you would like?*
- *Are you not well or is someone in your family not feeling so good?*

Sit on the mat or floor. Think of that thing and think of what you would like to replace it with. Take a few deep breaths in and out. Hold that intention with you as you start your yoga practice.

Are you a yogini or yogi?

- If you are a girl who does yoga you are called a yogini.
- If you are a boy who does yoga you are called a yogi.

1 | *On the first day I met him*
my yogi sent to me
a caterpillar singing loudly.

A Caterpillar Singing Loudly

Caterpillar, Pose of Eight points or Ashtang Pranam

(Ashtang = 8 and Pranam = Limb)

1 Lie on your belly with your forehead on the floor and your hands underneath the shoulders.

2 Tuck your toes under and stick your bottom in the air by walking your feet and knees forward towards your hips. Don't forget to put your chin on the floor. Breathe freely and normally

Question?

Can you figure out why it is called pose of eight points?

Eight parts of your body are in contact with the floor, two for your feet, two for your knees, one for your hands, one for your chest and one for your chin, makes a pose of eight points.

Answer

Benefits

- Strengthens neck & shoulders;
- Realigns the back;
- Increases energy in belly.

Empower Yourself!

Caterpillars represent transformation and change. Think about how you have changed and transformed over the years and as you hold the pose affirm "I believe in myself and I can achieve great things".

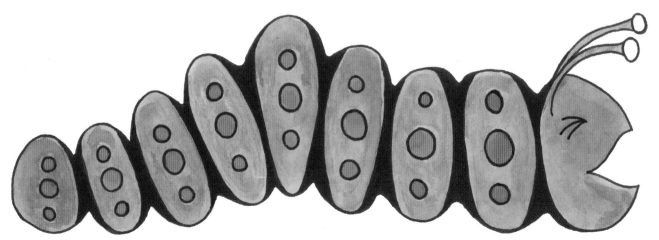

2

*On the second day I met him
my yogi sent to me
two hissing cobras.*

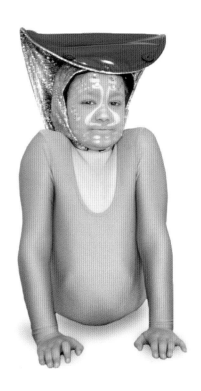

Two Hissing Cobras
Cobra or Bhujangasana (Bhujanga = Cobra and Asana = Pose)

1

2

1 Lie on your belly with your hands beneath your shoulders and forehead on the floor.

Breathing tip – Tuck your tongue behind your teeth and take a deep breathe in through your nose as you breathe out make a gentle hissing sound. See how long you can breathe out for without making yourself feel dizzy.

Benefits

- Strengthens the spine;
- Stretches chest, lungs, shoulders and belly;
- Raises energy and de-stresses.

2 On your next in-breath slowly trace a line on the floor with your nose and rise up into the mighty cobra. Try the breathing tip if you feel up to it.

Empower Yourself!

Many ancient cultures thought that cobras were powerful creatures that were there to protect and keep special places safe. Remember the inner cobra within you whenever you feel down and as you hold the pose affirm "I am special and worthy of protecting myself".

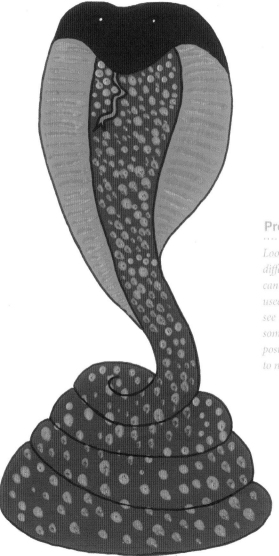

Project

Look up how many different snakes you can find that were used for protection and see if you can create some new snake yoga postures. Don't forget to name them!

3

On the third day I met him
my yogi sent to me
three stretched-out-dormice.

Three Stretched-Out-Dormice

Stretched-Out-Dormice, extended child, Balasana (Bala = child and Asana = pose)

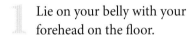

1 Lie on your belly with your forehead on the floor.

2 Breathe in, press-up and as you breathe out take your bottom to your heels. Remember to keep your dormouse arms stretched out in front of you. Pause and breathe deeply in this pose.

Challenge

See how long you can be still for in either extended dormouse or dormouse pose (see later section). Take deep-in and out-breathes. An in-breath and an out-breath count as one round see how long you can rest in this pose by counting the rounds of breath.

Benefits

- Stretches hips, thighs and ankles;
- Calms the mind and soothes the nerves.

Empower Yourself!

Dormice are quiet and shy creatures but don't be deceived as to thinking they are weak as they are incredibly strong. We all need time to be still, reflect and build our energy reserves. When you feel tired rest in dormouse pose and as you hold the pose affirm "I am calm, I am quiet and this will help me be strong for what I will do next."

A Caterpillar Singing Loudly

19

4 | *On the fourth day I met him*
my yogi sent to me
four happy cats.

Four Happy Cats
Happy Cat, Cat, Marjaryasana (Marjari = cat and Asana = posture)

1 Lie on your belly with either your forehead or cheek on the floor and hands beneath your shoulders.

2 Breathe in and come onto your hands and knees. Make sure the crown of your head and cat's tail point to the sky.

Benefits
- Stretches the back;
- Builds strength in the back and upper body;
- Gets energy flowing again.

Empower Yourself!
Imagine that you are a playful kitty cat and that the world around you is bright and exciting. Affirm to yourself as you hold the pose "May I always be playful and excited no matter what job I have to do".

5

*On the fifth day I met him
my yogi sent to me
five downward dogs.*

Five Downward Dogs

Downward Facing Dog, Adho Mukha Svanasana
(Adho = Downward, Mukha = Face and Svana = Dog and Asana = Pose)

1 Lie on your belly with your forehead on the floor and your hands beneath your shoulders. Don't forget to tuck your toes under.

2 Breathe in and press up strongly so that you look like a piece of wood. No bottoms in the air!

3 Breathe out and now take your bottom into the air. Open up your fingers and thumbs so that you have paws. Try to make your back really flat by pushing your belly to your thighs.

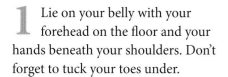

Benefits

- Stretches the back;
- Builds strength in the back and upper body;
- Gets energy flowing again.

Empower Yourself!

Imagine you are a playful puppy exploring the world and affirm to yourself as you hold the pose "I feel great! I am happy."

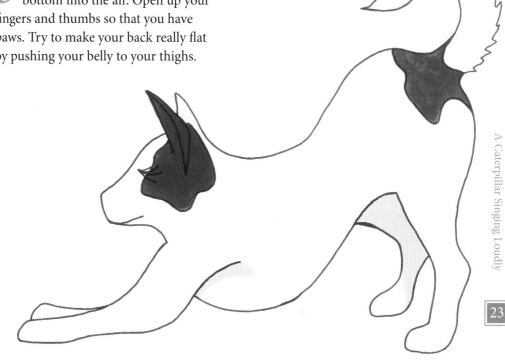

A Caterpillar Singing Loudly

6

On the sixth day I met him
my yogi sent to me
six crazy lizards.

Six Crazy Lizards
Crazy Lizard, Plank Pose or Adho Mukha Dandasana
(Adho = Downward, Mukha = Face, Danda = Staff and Asana = Pose)

1 Lie on your belly with your forehead on the floor, hands underneath the shoulders and toes tucked under.

2 Breathe in and push up strongly with your arms. No bottoms in the air! If you want to when you next breathe out stick your tongue out and hiss loudly!!

Benefits
- Tones and strengthens arms, wrists and back;
- Tones your belly.

Empower Yourself!
Lizards come in all shapes and sizes and have come up with some whacky, weird and wonderful ways to survive. Affirm to yourself as you hold the pose "I will survive and be positive no matter what life throws at me".

Project
....
Have a look at the great variety of lizards there are in the world. They really are quite spectacular. You may want to print some out if you are looking on the PC or cut them out if you are looking through a magazine. Make a collage and write how they are good at adapting and surviving.

A Caterpillar Singing Loudly

C7 *On the seventh day I met him
my yogi sent to me
seven swans-a-swimming.*

A Caterpillar Singing Loudly

Seven Swans-A-Swimming

This pose is traditionally called Pigeon Pose,

Kapotasana (Kapota = Pigeon and Asana = Pose)

1 Come into a kneeling pose.

2 Place both hands on the floor and as you breathe out slide your left leg back a comfortable distance.

3 Now see if you can balance by placing a crown on the top of your swan head. Now repeat on the other side so that you are balanced.

Why Do I Call It Swan Pose?

When I first started teaching children this pose. I would first do sleeping swan as they do in Yin Yoga and then we would come out of it and move into the traditionally named Pigeon Pose where I quite naturally called it "Swan Pose with a crown on its head". Sleeping swan and swan pose worked well together so it just stuck and the kids love it.

Project

Try out some different styles of yoga. Can you find out how to do sleeping swan?

Benefits

- Swan pose is excellent for opening up the hips;
- Opens the chest and shoulders;
- Develops concentration as you try to balance in the pose;
- Raises energy and de-stresses.

Empower Yourself!

Have you ever noticed how swans always look cool, calm and collected, even in the most challenging weather conditions? Affirm to yourself as you hold the pose "My thoughts are calm, I feel quiet and peaceful".

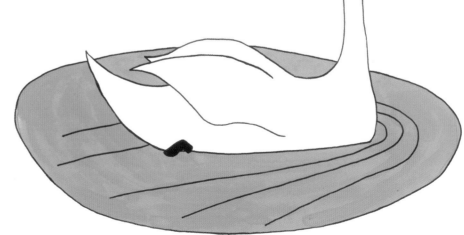

8 | *On the eighth day I met him my yogi sent to me eight festive camels.*

Eight Festive Camels

Camel Pose or Ustrasana (Ustra = Camel and Asana = Pose)

1 High kneeling pose.

2 Don't bend back just yet but place your hands on your lower back. Take a deep breath in and as you breathe out push your hips forward and tuck your chin to your chest.

3 This is how you look from the front. Try and squeeze your shoulders together and get your elbows towards each other. Try to also keep your hips above your knees.

Tip:

After you have held camel for a while it is important that you rest in dormouse. Camel is a back bend and dormouse is a forward bend. When I teach I usually follow one after the other because the back loves it!

Benefits

- Stretches the whole of the front of the body;
- Strengthens the back;
- Gently massages the organs in your tummy.

Empower Yourself!

Camels are really good at storing water and surviving in the heat. Affirm to yourself as you hold the pose "My body is filled with good thoughts, good words and good actions".

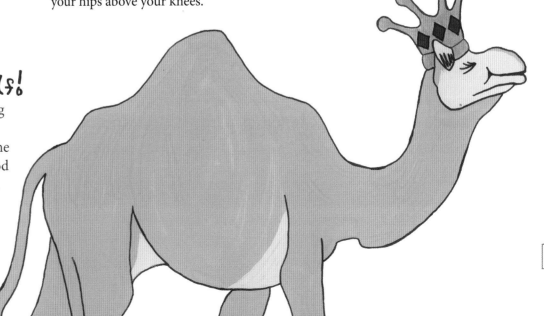

9

*On the ninth day I met him
my yogi sent to me
nine cheetahs running.*

Nine Cheetahs Running

Cheetah, Runner Pose, low lunge or Premasana (Prem = low lunge and Asana = Pose)

1

2

1 Start in high kneeling pose.

2 Take a breath in and step forward with your right leg as you breathe out place your hands onto the floor. Now roar mightily like the cheetah within you!

Deepen the pose – As you practice this pose try to take it deeper by stretching your back leg further and also try to lengthen through the spine by taking the crown of your head towards the sky. Remember take it easy and make sure it feels comfortable!

Benefits

- Opens the hips;
- Stretches the legs;
- Lengthens the spine.

Empower Yourself!

Cheetahs are fast, flexible, strong and sensitive. Affirm to yourself as you hold the pose "I will try to do my yoga practice as best as I can so that I can keep my mind and body fast, strong and flexible".

A Caterpillar Singing Loudly

31

10

*On the tenth day I met him
my yogi sent to me
ten trees-a-swaying.*

Ten Trees-A-Swaying

Tree Pose or Vrksasana (Vrksa = tree and asana = pose)

1 Stand in Mountain pose. Make sure your feet are hip-width apart, your arms are by your sides and you are standing tall and strong.

2 Take the weight onto your left leg, focus on a point that does not move and when you next breathe in simultaneously raise your right leg and arms. Right foot is placed on the left leg and right knee goes out to the side while your palms touch above your head. Repeat on other side.

Benefits

- Strengthens the legs and the spine;
- Improves balance and concentration;
- Reduces flat feet.

Empower Yourself!

Trees are always giving and sharing with us and nature. They give us shade, oxygen, they keep the earth fertile and animals build their homes in them. Today take the time to walk in nature or sit in your garden. Breathe in the fresh air. Once you have done that pick some flowers, leaves, pine cones, pebbles, twigs, conkers etc or go inside and make a card. Give that gift to someone. See how that makes you feel.

Project

When the Autumn leaves begin to fall go out and collect some. Take them home, create a collage or if you have a laminate machine (make sure you are working with a grown-up because these get hot) laminate your autumn leaves and turn them into a mobile. Or when you practice your tree you can stick the leaves to your body.

Challenge

How long can you hold your tree for? Begin counting, focus your mind and work with the breath. What number did you get up to?

Fun

Now you may want to be a hopping tree. Hop around the room for as long as you can but don't forget to do both sides.

A Caterpillar Singing Loudly

33

11

On the eleventh day I met him
my yogi sent to me
eleven surfers surfing.

If you are boy that surfs you are called Surfer Dude and if you are a girl that surfs you are called Surfer Dudess.

Eleven Surfers Surfing

Surfer Dude or Dudess, Warrior Pose

Virabhadrasana II (Virabhadra = the name of a fierce warrior and Asana = Pose)

1 Stand in Mountain pose. Make sure your feet are hip-width apart, your arms are by your sides and you are standing tall and strong.

2 Widen your stance or make a big gap between your feet. Don't be silly it should not be too big!

3 Turn your right foot to the right and adjust your left slightly.

4 Check your feet are in the right place (or aligned correctly).

5 Take a breathe in and raise your arms to shoulder height when you breathe out bend your right knee and look to the right. Repeat to the other side.

Benefits

- Strengthens the legs and arms;
- Stretches the legs, lungs and shoulders;
- Increases energy.

Empower Yourself!

Everyone has a warrior inside them. Think of the warrior inside you and as you hold the pose affirm "I am strong and courageous!"

Tip

Try to relax your shoulders as you breathe deeply in and out but still keep your arms shoulder height and strong.

Deepen the pose:
As you practice try and get your legs wider and sink more deeply into the posture. **Remember not to over do it!** As you hold feel the strength and power in your body! You feel and look great!

A Caterpillar Singing Loudly

12

*On the twelfth day I met him
my yogi sent to me
twelve dancers dancing.*

Twelve Dancers Dancing

Dancer Pose, Lord of the Dance Pose, Natarajasana
(Nata = Dancer, Raja = King/Lord and Asana = Pose)

1 Stand in Mountain pose. Make sure your feet are hip-width apart, your arms are by your sides and you are standing tall and strong.

2 Grab hold of your right foot and create a hand gesture of your choice take a breathe in and as you breathe out stretch forward with your arm and take your foot away from your bottom. Repeat on other side.

Did you know?

Hasta Mudras known as hand gestures are a type of yoga for the hands. They are probably more powerful than yoga postures.

Hand gesture 1: Simply have your palm facing you.

Hand gesture 2: Create the pose of wisdom called the Jnana Mudra by allowing your thumb and index fingers to touch.

Hand gesture 3: Create the Deer Mudra called Hamsasya by allowing your middle and ring finger to rest on your thumb, make sure your index and little finger point to the sky. Do you see how it looks like a deer?

Benefits

- Strengthens the legs and back;
- Stretches the chest and shoulders;
- Improves balance and concentration.

Empower Yourself!

Lord of the Dance pose is about bringing strength and grace into your body and mind. As you hold the pose affirm to yourself "I am strong and beautiful."

Project:

After you have practiced the dancer you may also like to try these mudras out in a seated position. See what happens. How do they make you feel? Write it down.

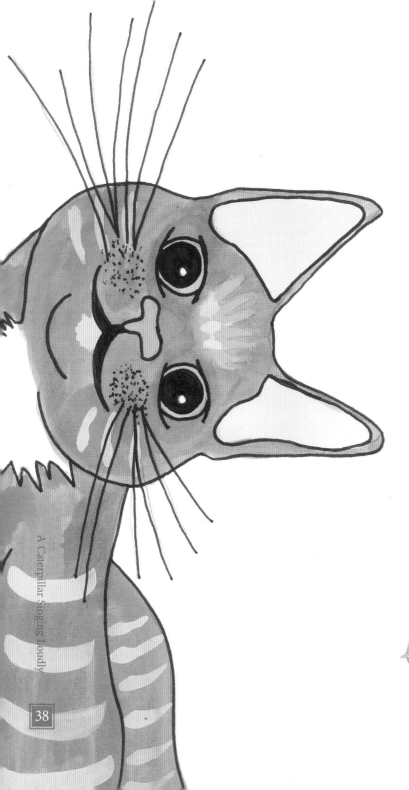

How Do I Get From One Pose To The Next?

For most of the sequence it is quite easy to figure out how to get from one pose to the next. However, there are a few postures where it is a bit more difficult to figure out the transitions.

In this section we will show you how to change from one posture into the next. As you go up the sequence (from the first day to the twelfth day you met him) you always start off with the caterpillar pose so I will explain the transitions for the following:

- Caterpillar into Swan;
- Caterpillar into Camel;
- Caterpillar into Cheetah;
- Caterpillar into Tree;
- Caterpillar into Surfer and
- Caterpillar into Dancer.

As you go down the sequence you need to know the transitions for the following postures:

- Camel into Swan;
- Cheetah into Camel;
- Tree into Cheetah;
- Surfer into Tree and
- Dancer into Surfer.

Caterpillar into Swan

  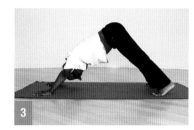  

1 Caterpillar pose.

2 Breathe in press up into crazy lizard.

3 Breathe out go into downward facing dog.

4 Breathe in bring the right knee between your hands and go into swan. Take a breathe out.

5 Breathe in and place your crown on your swans head.

Caterpillar into Camel

1 Caterpillar pose.

2 Breathe in into happy cat.

3 Breathe out high kneeling pose.

4 Place your hands on your lower back breathe in and on an out breath

push your hips forward and tuck your chin to your chest.

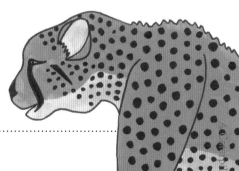

Caterpillar into Cheetah

1 Caterpillar pose.

2 Breathe in into happy cat.

3 Breathe out into high kneeling pose. Breathe in into your spine.

4 Breathe out and step forward with your right leg into Cheetah.

Caterpillar into Tree

1 Caterpillar pose.

2 Breathe in into happy cat.

3 Breathe out into high kneeling pose.

4 Breathe in mountain pose. Take a breath out.

5 Breathe in turn into tree pose with your right leg leading.

Caterpillar into Surfer

1 Caterpillar pose.

2 Breathe in into happy cat.

3 Breathe out into high kneeling pose.

4 Breathe in mountain pose.

5 Breathe out step forward with right leg and raise your arms to shoulder height.

Caterpillar into Dancer

1 Caterpillar pose.

2 Breathe in into happy cat.

3 Breathe out into high kneeling pose.

4 Breathe in mountain pose. Take a breath out.

5 Breathe in take your right leg back and your left arm forward. Don't forget a hand gesture.

Transitions For Going Down The Sequence (Remember your left leg leads)

Camel into Swan

1 Camel Pose.

2 Breathe out kneeling posture.

3 Breathe in keep your left leg where it is and as you breathe out slide your right leg back.

4 Breathe in place the crown upon your head.

Cheetah into Camel

1 Cheetah pose with the left leg forward.

2 Breathe in and turn into high kneeling pose.

3 Place your hands on the lower back and as you breathe out push your hips forward and tuck your chin under.

Tree into Cheetah

1 Tree 1 with left foot leading.

2 Breathe in step forward with left leg.

3 Breathe out place right knee onto the floor.

4 Breathe in lengthen through the spine.

41

Surfer into Tree

1 Surfer pose with left leg leading.

2 Breathe in step forward with right leg into mountain pose. Breathe out.

3 On your next in-breath go into tree pose with the left leg leading.

Dancer into Surfer

1 Dancer pose with left leg back.

2 Breathe out step forward with the left leg into Surfer Pose.

A Caterpillar Singing Loudly. The Full Sequence

You are now a grand master yogini and yogi. You have practiced all the postures and are ready to do the sequence. Take your time, take it steady and remember to have fun with it.

…a caterpillar singing loudly

…two hissing cobras

…three stretched-out dormice

…four happy cats

…five downward-dogs

…six crazy lizards

On the first day I met him my yogi sent to me
a caterpillar singing loudly.

On the second day I met him my yogi sent to me
two hissing cobras.

On the third day I met him my yogi sent to me
three stretched out dormice.

On the fourth day I met him my yogi sent to me
four happy cats.

On the fifth day I met him my yogi sent to me
five downward dogs.

On the sixth day I met him my yogi sent to me
six crazy lizards.

…seven swans-a-swimming

…eight festive camels

…nine cheetahs running

…ten trees-a-swaying

…eleven surfers surfing

…twelve dancers dancing

On the seventh day I met him my yogi sent to me
seven swans-a-swimming.

On the eighth day I met him my yogi sent to me
eight festive camels.

On the ninth day I met him my yogi sent to me
nine cheetahs running.

On the tenth day I met him my yogi sent to me
ten trees-a-swaying.

On the eleventh day I met him my yogi sent to me
eleven surfers surfing.

On the twelfth day I met him my yogi sent to me
twelve dancers dancing.

Challenge!

It is important that you try and balance both sides of your body. So as you go up the sequence your right leg leads and as you go down the sequence your left leg leads. Don't get hung-up on this if you don't get it, with time you will master it like you have everything else.

Some Other Asanas You May Wish To Try

In the photos where the children have their face painted and the "starring" child has their costume on you may notice the other children doing some different postures.

Once you have become a master yogini or yogi of the sequence you may wish to try some of the other postures you see in the photos.

An explanation of what they are and how to get into them follows.

Advanced Cobra

1 Lie on your belly with your hands beneath your shoulders and forehead on the floor.

2 On your next in-breath slowly trace a line on the floor with your nose and rise up into the mighty cobra.

3 Try and get your head to your feet.

Dormouse

1 Lie on your belly with your hands beneath your shoulders and forehead on the floor.

2 Breathe in come up into happy cat and as you breathe out sink into stretched out dormouse

3 Tuck your dormouse arms by the sides of your body. See how long you can stay still for, use your breath to help you count.

Sad Cat

1 Start on your hands. Breathe in and lengthen through the spine. Make sure the crown of your head and cat's tail point to the sky.

2 As you breathe out arch into sad cat pose.

Challenge:

....

see how many happy and sad cats you can do with the breath. No whiplashing cats please.

Weaving Cat

1 Start on your hands. Breathe in and lengthen through the spine. Make sure the crown of your head and cat's tail point to the sky.

2 Become aware of your right arm and as you breathe out weave your arm beneath your left and place your cheek on the floor.

3 Become aware of your left arm and as you breathe in raise it up to sky. Come back into happy cat pose and do the other side.

Benefits

- Stretches out shoulders;
- Builds strength in back;
- Stretches out the pecs and upper arms.

Downward Facing Dog Split

1 Lie on your belly with your hands beneath your shoulders and forehead on the floor.

2 Breathe in and press up into crazy lizard pose.

3 Breathe out and turn into downward facing dog by taking your bottom to the air.

4 Breathe in and raise your right leg up, breathe out place it on the floor and then repeat on other side.

Forearm Plank (Crazy Lizard)

1 Lie on your belly with your hands beneath your shoulders and forehead on the floor. Tuck your toes under.

2 Place your forearms on the floor and as you breathe in press up nice and strongly.

Supine Plank (Crazy Lizard)

1 Sit on your bottom with your legs stetched out in front of you. Place your hands on the floor behind you with your finger tips facing forward.

2 When you next breathe in press up with your arms and take your bottom off the floor. Try and keep yourself nice and straight and if you can flatten your feet onto the floor.

A good tip is to remember to squeeze your bottom muscles.

New Word!

*Supine means lying on your back with your face looking up at the **pine** trees. If you remember pine trees you should remember Supine and also which way to lye down.*

The opposite of supine is prone which means lying on your belly.

One-armed plank, side plank pose (Crazy Lizard)

1 Lie on your belly with your hands beneath your shoulders and forehead on the floor. Tuck your toes under.

2 Breathe in and press up with your arms. Try and keep yourself nice and straight. No sagging at the hips and no bottom in the air. Take a breath out.

3 When you next breathe in take the weight onto your right arm and stretch your left arm up to the sky. Try and keep both feet on top of each other or if you prefer you can have one slightly forward. Repeat on other side.

Swan with a gentle backbend

1 Begin in kneeling pose.

2 Take a breath in and as you breathe out slide your left leg back.

3 Place your hands on your lower back and as you breathe in push your hips forward and look up towards the sky. Repeat on other side.

Benefits

- Opens up the hips;
- Stretches the front of the body and internal organs;
- Strengthens the back;
- Improves balance and concentration.

Advanced Camel Warning – this is a very strong pose and it should feel comfortable. If it does not feel comfortable then you should not be doing it.

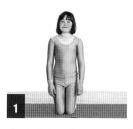

1 Begin in the high kneeling pose and keep the tops of your feet flat on the floor. Keep your knees hip width a part.

2 Place both hands on your ankles or feet, take a breath in and as you breathe out arch back and also take your head back.

3 How it looks from the front. Remember to follow it with a forward bend.

Benefits

- Stretches the front of the body;
- Very good for rounded shoulders and for people with asthma;
- Strengthens the back.

Half Crescent Moon (Cheetah)

1 Begin in the high kneeling pose.

2 Breathe in step forward with your right leg. Take a breath out.

3 Breathe in take both arms above your head and allow your palms to touch, at the same time look up to the sky. Repeat on other side.

Benefits

- Stretches the hip flexes;
- Builds strength in arms and back;
- Good for developing balance and concentration.

Cheetah sky and earth twist

1 Begin in the high kneeling pose.

2 Breathe in step forward with your right leg.

3 As you breathe out place your right hand on the floor. When you are ready to breathe in raise your left arm up to the sky and follow that movement so that you too are looking at the sky. Repeat on other side.

Benefits

- Stretches hip flexes;
- Builds strength in arms and back;
- Detoxes the body by twisting the internal organs.

Twisted Dragon (Cheetah)

1 Begin in the high kneeling pose.

2 Breathe in step forward with your right leg.

Tip…Before you twist make sure you have chosen the correct elbow.

3 As you breathe out take your left elbow and place it on your right knee. Both palms together so that you have created a birds beak. On an in-breath twist and look up at the right elbow. Repeat on other side.

Benefits

- Stretches out the hip flexes;
- Builds strength in back;
- Detoxes the body and develops balance and concentration.

Tree 1

1 Stand in mountain pose with either your palms together or by your side.

2 As you breathe in place the heel of your right foot on the big toe of your left foot. At the same time palms touch above your head.

Challenge

See if you can link all the movements with your breath and hold for a few moments.

Tree 3

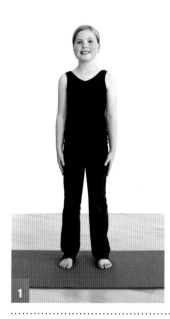

1 Stand in mountain pose with either your palms together or by your side.

Tip

To get your leg up high you may need to use your hand to help you get it up there. If you find you are slipping try it with shorts on. Skin on skin acts like glue and minimises slipping.

2 As you breathe in raise your right leg up as high as you can and at the same time get your palms to touch on top of your head.

Tree 4

This posture has been added for a bit of fun…it is quite a difficult one but I thought you might like to experiment with it like Caitlin is doing.

1 Stand in mountain pose with either your palms together or by your side.

2 Breathe normally as this tree is quite a challenging pose. As you try and balance on your left leg, you take your right leg up to the left hip, you then try and grab hold of the big toe of your right foot with the right hand. Once you have mastered it you may want to try stretching your left arm up to the sky.

Yogic Nap Time (Yoga Nidra)

WOW! You have completed your yoga practice. You should be feeling really good and very proud with yourself. It is really important that you now lie down to relax or have a yogic nap. Put on some nice relaxing music, snuggle with a blanket, place your head on a pillow and make sure you have your favourite nap toy or blanket with you.

I'd like you to be as still as a stone, as quiet as a stone and as light as a feather. To help you, use your breath, breathe in and out through your different body parts.

How do you do this? In your mind think of the body part I am talking about, breathe into it and then breathe out from it.

Here let me help

Think of your feet – breathe into them and then breathe out from them, relax your feet.

Think of your legs – breathe into them and then breathe out from them, soften your legs.

Think of your hips – breathe into them and then breathe out from them, relax your hips.

Think of you back – breathe into your back and then breathe out from it, soften your back.

Think of your belly – breathe into your belly and as you breathe out from your belly make it soft.

Think of your chest – breathe into your chest and breathe out from it, relax your chest.

Think of your hands and arms – breathe into them and as you breathe out soften your hands and arms.

Think of your shoulders – breathe into them and as you breathe out relax them.

Think of your neck and throat – breathe into them and as you breathe out relax them.

Think of your head – breathe into your head and as you breathe out relax it.

Think of your beautiful face – breathe into your beautiful face and as you breathe out relax your beautiful face.

Think of the whole of your body – breathe into the whole of your body and breathe out from the whole of your body, make sure you relax every single part of you.

As you lie there relaxing and letting go imagine a beautiful summers night, you are lying outside on the earth and you are watching a deep indigo sky covered in stars and a big fat moon.

As you rest there you are completely safe, no one can harm you, you gently sigh out with the happiness you feel at this moment in time. You feel the earth beneath you cradling you and filling you with love and peace.

You look at the sky above you and see all your dreams in the stars and in the moon. With the earth giving you strength and courage you are confident that your dreams will come true. With each round of the breath you draw in the star and moon light a little bit deeper into your body and you place those precious dreams in your heart.

You keep taking deep breaths in and out until you become a reflection of the night sky. You are star light and moon dust. You feel the whole of your body gently vibrating with silvery white light and you feel your dreams gently beginning to unfold and become true. You rest deeply and you affirm to yourself

"I am filled with courage and confidence and all my dreams will come true in the fullness of time".

Allow yourself to rest for as long as you desire. When your beautiful body is ready to move, deepen your breath, wiggle your toes and fingers, have a nice stretch and quietly come up into a seated position. Don't rush to get up and start doing things, just spend a few moments and feel how you are feeling now.

A Caterpillar Singing Loudly

Why is it important to have a yogic nap?

During yoga nidra your body has the time to take the energy you have created through your yoga practice and as you rest it will repair cells, create new links in your brain called neural pathways and fill your spine with a special fluid called cerebrospinal fluid. As the energy settles deep in your body your concentration will increase, you get rid of any remaining toxins and you fill your body with nutrients and vitality.

It is said that ten minutes of relaxation is the equivalent of two hours of sleep. Learning to relax is also important so that you can deal with all of the challenges life throws at you in a positive way.

Yoga Nidra – Nidra translates as sleep but yoga nidra is conscious sleep, sleep without falling asleep.

Project
....
After your yogic nap you may want to write down how you are feeling and what has changed just like you did for the project in the first section.

51

Facts About A Caterpillar Singing Loudly

Did you know that once you have completed this sequence once, you will have done all of these!

1. caterpillar pose 12 times;

2. cobra pose 11 times;

3. stretched out dormouse 10 times;

4. happy cat 9 times;

5. downward facing dog 8 times;

6. crazy lizard 7 times;

7. swan 6 times;

8. camel 5 times;

9. cheetah 4 times;

10. tree 3 times;

11. surfer 2 times;

12. dancer 2 times.

That is a grand total of 79 postures! You are officially a Grand Master Yogini or Yogi!

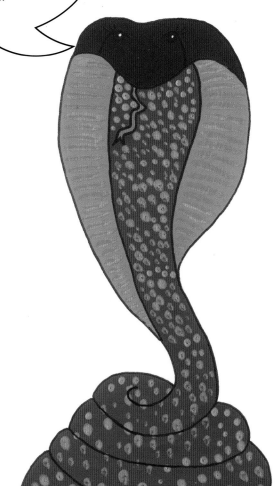

I hope you have enjoyed your yogic adventure.
We look forward to having more with you!

Project 1

Make yourself a yoga badge that you can wear and be proud off for your great achievement. Be creative put your favourite pose on it or the one you found the hardest to master and don't forget to include the title Grand Master Yogini or Yogi.

Project 2

Time yourself, next time you do the sequence see how long it takes you to do it at a normal pace. You may then want to see how long it takes you to do it slowly as you try and hold the postures for 5 to 10 seconds.

Project 3

Write down all the unusual words you have come across in this book. See if you remember their meaning, try to use them in another sentence and check if you know how to spell them.

Project 4

Now that you are a Grand Master Yogini or Yogi you will wish to share your knowledge with family and friends. Have a Caterpillar Singing Loudly Party and teach them how to do the sequence.

Francesca
Age 4

Favourite Pose – Tree. I like yoga because we play games & do crafts.

Jonny
Age 5

Favourite Pose – Bridge. I like the yoga postures, games, yogic nap and yoga is fun.

Sahara
Age 9

Favourite Pose – Cheetah. I like yoga because it is relaxing and fun.

Morgan
Age 11

Favourite Pose – Crazy Lizard. I like yoga because it relaxes and calms me. It is also good to do stretching.

Resian
Age 8

Favourite Pose – Dormouse. I like yoga because it makes me feel relaxed.

Hayden
Age 7

Favourite Pose – Swan. I like yoga because it is very relaxing and fun.

Elise
Age 8

Favourite Pose – Locust. I just like it cause I like it! Yoga is fun and it makes me able to do more things because I become more flexible.

Alexandra
Age 10

Favourite Pose – Snail aka plough. Yoga is nice and relaxing and calms you if you have had a bad day.

Caitlin
Age 10

Favourite Pose – Headstand. I like yoga because it is energetic but doesn't wear you out so you can do it for a long time. It is quite exciting.

Lily
Age 9

Favourite Pose – Cobra. Yoga is relaxing! I like the games & it is really enjoyable.

Cenya
Age 9

Favourite Pose – Camel. Yoga makes you feel really relaxed. The breath makes you feel nice. It is really fun doing all the different poses.

Sophia
Age 9

Favourite Pose – Shoulder Stand. Yoga is fun & exciting. I like the games & the yogic nap. It is relaxing, gets me away from home and the yoga postures make me happy.

A Caterpillar Singing Loudly

The Shanti Path - Om Dyau, Shanthir anta rikshagoon, Shanthi pritharvi, Shanthir apah, Shanthir oshadhayah, Shanthi vanaspatayah, Shanthi vishvedevah, Shanthi brahma, Shanthi sarvagoon, Shanthi shanthir eva, Shanthi sama, Shanthir edhi, Om Shanthi Shanthi Shanthi.

The Peace Path (The Shanti Path)

Let there be peace in the heavens
Let there be peace in the sky and the earth
Let there be peace in the water
And in the forests and trees
May there be peace in the heart and mind
Of every living thing
Let there be peace on the earth
And may we realise that peace
Peace Peace Peace

With Metta (With Loving Kindness)

My gratitude and love go to all the wonderful children who inspired me and gave me the courage to write this book. To all the amazing yoginis and yogis who participated in the making of this book. Your cooperation, patience and understanding over the two day photo shoot was gratefully received. To you the reader for taking the time to read this book and cultivate yourself into a Grand Master Yogini or Yogi.

To all my students who have inspired and guided my teaching. I would also like to thank my yoga teachers Wendy Faulknall, Susie Tinsley and Janey Fitzerald and all the amazing teachings from the Dru Yoga School. Thank you Dru Yoga Teachers for sharing your wisdom and deep insight of yoga.

My heartfelt blessings and well wishes go to Ruthie for her amazing talent in costume design and the beautiful illustrations for this book, Sarah for her beautiful eyes in taking the photographs for this book, Liz for her stunning skill in face painting the children for this book and Jason for his incredible graphic design skills for this book. A great big thank you to Vincent who manages the Sharrow Performing Arts Space where the photos were taken, to Janet and Deborah for keeping the space beautifully clean for our use and for also putting up with some weird demands over the two day photo shoot.

I would also like to extend my thanks to my mother, father, sister and brother without them I would not be the person who I am today. Thank you family for your tolerance, understanding, love of all things natural, organic, simple and for letting me be who I am.

My heartfelt thanks and love go to Joan Duxbury for setting up my first yoga class all those years ago. Without her relentless support and belief in me I would not have achieved all that I have done today. Finally, to my beautiful partner, Ben Major, without him I would not be whole. Thank you for your quiet continued support where you have tolerated even my most wackiest yoga ideas without criticism. You have allowed me to bloom like no other.

A Caterpillar Singing Loudly

Joanna Bertzeletos has been a student of yoga for almost 20 years and teaching yoga for nearly 10 years. Jo would like to share yoga with you because simply it has helped her so much in her own life. It has helped Jo to cultivate peace, gratitude, forgiveness and compassion. Yoga continues to help her cultivate these qualities and other areas of herself.

Jo believes that once you start on your yogic adventure that you too will begin to feel its magic working within you. With time Jo hopes that the world will then become a reflection of us. Jo teaches a range of adult and children's yoga classes, shares yoga in schools and with people with special needs. Jo has many favourite yoga poses but if she had to choose one it would be downward facing dog.

www.yoganaturesheffield.org.uk

Sarah Ingolfsdottir is a Sheffield based photographer who has enjoyed 10 years of creating images that capture the essence of the subject with which she works. A passion for photographing people has led to a successful wedding photogrpahy career, resulting primarliy from a strength in building trust and forming relationships with both her clients and subjects. As well as working in travel photography for one of the world's leading mountaineering companies, Sarah's also enjoying teaching photography at the local, co-founded photography school called Sharrow Photo School.

Sarah's favourite yoga pose is the fish. For more information and to contact Sarah go to:

www.ingophoto.co.uk

Ruthie Ford is a freelance textiles artist. Ruthie creates crochet and fabric craft installations for festivals, events and exhibitions as well as working on occasional textiles and illustration commissions such as this one!

Ruthie has attended Jo's yoga classes for the past 3 years and her favourite yoga pose is the cobra. For more information about the lovely Ruthie please visit:

www.ruthieford.blogspot.com

Liz Searle has been enjoying facepainting adults and children for four years now, and is developing new ideas as part of costumes for festivals and performances. An artist, she also works in sculpture, textiles and on paper. She loves yoga and her favourite pose is the tree.

liz.searle@hotmail.co.uk

Jason Major is a Sheffield based Graphic/web designer and artist specializing in cost effective web design and logo packages tailored for business Start-ups and small to medium sized businesses.

Visit MajorMajordesign.com to view portfolio and see packages.

MAJOR MAJOR design.com

A Caterpillar Singing Loudly

58